SUPER SHARKS

written by Annabel Griffin
illustrated by Rose Wilkinson

Copyright © 2023 Hungry Tomato Ltd

First published in 2023 by Hungry Tomato Ltd
F15, Old Bakery Studios, Blewetts Wharf, Malpas Road, Truro, Cornwall, TR1 1QH, UK.

No part of this publication may be reproduced, stored in a retrieval system, or transmitted in any form or by any means, electronic, mechanical, photocopying, recording, or otherwise, without prior written permission of the copyright owner.

A CIP catalogue record for this book is available from the British Library.

ISBN 978-1-915461-71-1

Printed in China

Discover more at
www.hungrytomato.com

CONTENTS

SUPER SHARKS	4	SUPERSIZE CHART	18
GREAT WHITE SHARK	6	SUPER SHARK FACTS	20
BASKING SHARK	8	GLOSSARY	22
GREAT HAMMERHEAD	10	INDEX	23
WHALE SHARK	12		
GREENLAND SHARK	14		
GLOW IN THE DARK SHARKS	16		

Words in **bold** can be found in the glossary.

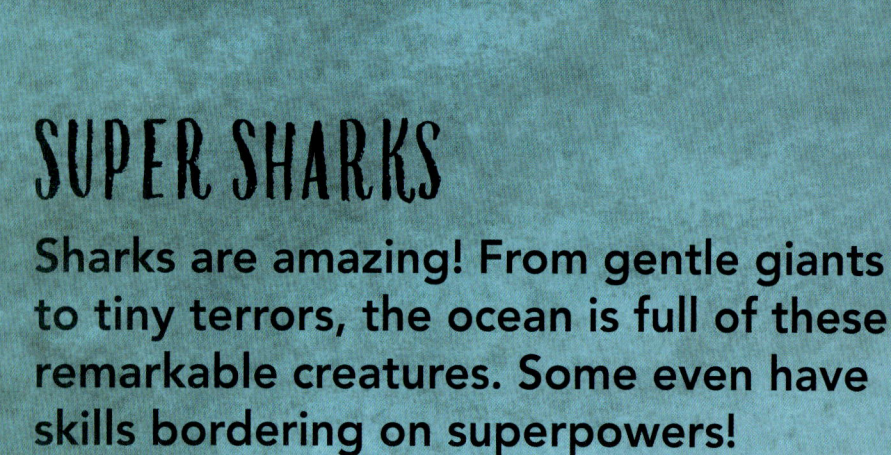

SUPER SHARKS

Sharks are amazing! From gentle giants to tiny terrors, the ocean is full of these remarkable creatures. Some even have skills bordering on superpowers!

Supersizes

There are over 500 different types of shark. They come in lots of different shapes and sizes.

Dwarf lanternshark: The World's Smallest Shark

Whale shark: The World's Largest Shark

Tiger shark

Super old

Sharks have been around for millions of years, and some haven't changed much in that time. What's more, one shark can live longer than any other animal on Earth!

Greenland shark

Super senses

Sharks have amazingly sharp senses to help them hunt for food in the water. They even have an extra special sixth sense!

Great white shark

GREAT WHITE SHARK

When you think of a shark, it's probably the image of a great white that comes to mind.

A great size
Great whites are the largest **predatory** fish on Earth. They can grow to around 6 m (20 feet) long.

Hungry hunters

A great white's diet includes other sharks, fish, shellfish, sea birds, seals, sea lions, and even some whales.

Big splash

They sometimes jump right out of the water when chasing their **prey.**

Humans not on the menu

On the very rare occasion that a great white bites a human, it usually spits them back out. They probably don't think we taste very nice!

BASKING SHARK

These sharks might look scary, with their big gaping mouths, but they are actually completely harmless.

Second prize
The basking shark is the world's second largest fish. They are usually around 8 m (26 feet) long.

Big mouth, tiny food
They mostly eat tiny sea creatures called *zooplankton*, but sometimes catch small fish too.

Lazy diners

Basking sharks don't hunt for food. They just swim around with their mouths wide open and wait for dinner to swim in.

Down the hatch

Their style of eating is called *filter feeding*. Their large **gills** are specially designed to let water out, while trapping any food.

gills

GREAT HAMMERHEAD SHARK

There are nine different types of hammerhead shark. They all have extra wide heads. The *great hammerhead* is the biggest of them all.

Stinging snack

Hammerheads love to eat stingrays. They use their big heads to pin them to the ocean floor.

Why the wide face?
The wide shape of their head allows them to see all around them at once.

Lone rangers
They are big loners and will travel long distances on their own.

Low swimmers
They spend a lot of time swimming along the bottom of the ocean, looking for food.

WHALE SHARK

Introducing the world's biggest fish! The largest known whale shark was over 18 m (59 feet) long. That's almost as long as a bowling lane!

Gentle giants

Whale sharks are harmless to humans. They are filter feeders, and only eat plankton, krill and small fish.

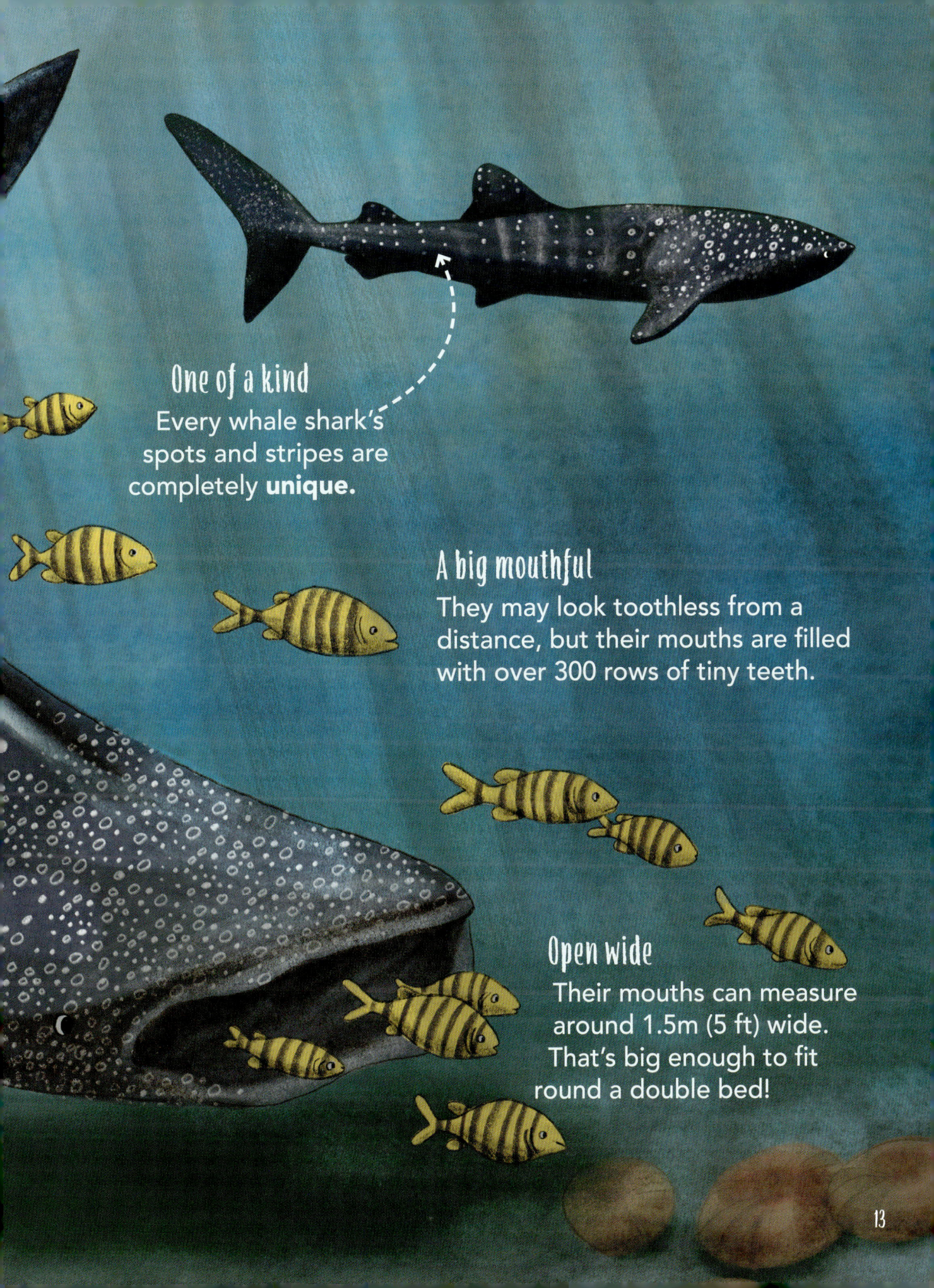

One of a kind
Every whale shark's spots and stripes are completely **unique.**

A big mouthful
They may look toothless from a distance, but their mouths are filled with over 300 rows of tiny teeth.

Open wide
Their mouths can measure around 1.5m (5 ft) wide. That's big enough to fit round a double bed!

GREENLAND SHARK

These large sharks are found in the freezing waters of the Arctic Ocean and the North Atlantic.

Old timers

Greenland sharks have one of the longest **lifespans** of any creature on Earth. Some scientists think that some of them have lived to be over 400 years old!

Frozen fish

Their flesh contains special chemicals that stop their bodies from freezing in the cold water. They also make them poisonous to eat.

Bad company

Most Greenland sharks have **parasites** hanging from their eyes. These tiny sea creatures make them go blind. Luckily the sharks can use their other senses to get around.

Slow and steady

They swim very slowly to save energy in the cold. They usually travel at under one mile per hour!

GLOW IN THE DARK SHARKS

Some sharks have an amazing superpower... they can glow in the dark!

Why glow?

There are different reasons why sharks might glow. It could attract prey, scare off predators, be used as **camouflage**, or for communicating with other sharks.

Kitefin shark

Big and bright

The kitefin shark is the largest-known **luminous** fish. It can grow to as large as 180 cm (5.9 feet) long.

Ninja lanternshark

Chain catshark

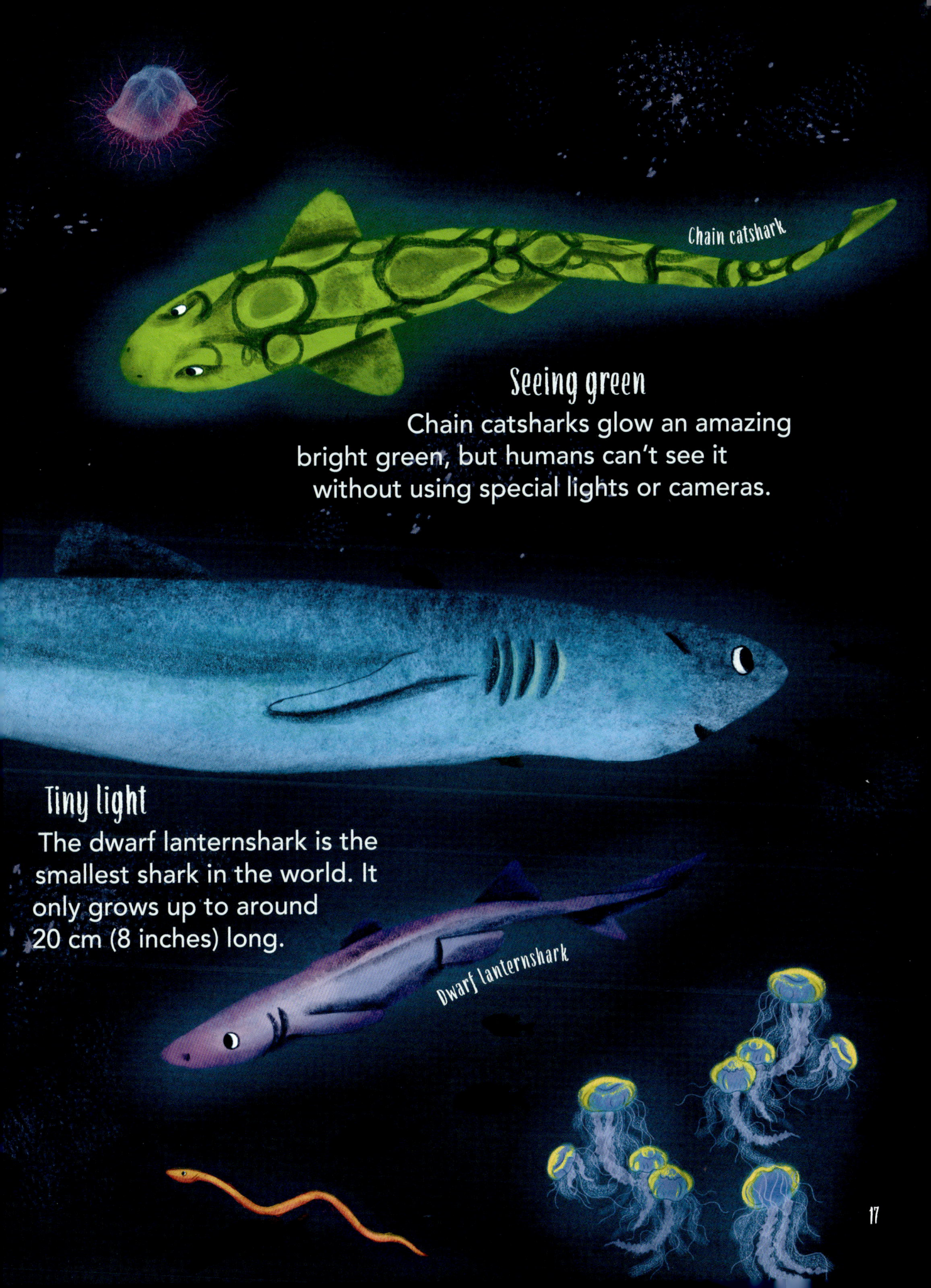

Seeing green
Chain catsharks glow an amazing bright green, but humans can't see it without using special lights or cameras.

Tiny light
The dwarf lanternshark is the smallest shark in the world. It only grows up to around 20 cm (8 inches) long.

Dwarf lanternshark

SUPERSIZE CHART

Sharks come in lots of different sizes. Some are small enough to hold in your hand, while others are as big as a school bus! This chart shows the size difference of the sharks in this book, and how they compare to humans.

Basking shark
7-8.5m (23-28 fe

Great white shark
3.5-4.9m (11-16 feet)

Ninja lanternshark
46-50cm (18-20 inches)

Chain catshark
38-52cm (14-20 inches)

Whale shark
8-14.5m (26-48 feet)

1 meter (3.3 feet)

Kitefin shark
1.0-1.4m (3.3-4.6 feet)

Great hammerhead shark
3.5-4.6m (11-15 feet)

Greenland shark
2.4-4.8m (8-15.7 feet)

Dwarf lanternshark
16-20cm (6-8 inches)

19

SUPER SHARK FACTS

Who's fastest?
The fastest shark in the world is the shortfin mako shark. It can swim up to 60 miles per hour!

Shortfin mako shark

Change your stripes
When they are young, zebra sharks are covered in black and white stripes. As they grow up, their patterns change from stripes to spots! Adults look more like leopards than zebras.

An adult zebra shark

Who's the daddy?

It's incredibly rare, but some female sharks are able to have babies on their own, without the help of a male!

Shark pups

The biggest ever

The largest shark of all time was the megalodon. At between 15–18m (50–60 feet), they were three times the size of a great white! But don't worry, they've been **extinct** for around 3.6 million years.

Comparison of a megalodon tooth and a great white shark tooth.

GLOSSARY

camouflage
To look like your surroundings, to help you stay hidden.

extinct
When a type of plant or animal no longer exists anywhere on Earth.

gills
A body part that sharks, and other fish, use to breathe underwater.

lifespans
The length of time that someone or something is alive for.

luminous
Something that shines light or glows.

parasites
Living things that live on or inside another living thing to survive.

predatory
Hunting and killing other animals for food. Animals that do this are called predators.

prey
An animal that is hunted and killed by other animals for food.

unique
Being the only one of its kind.

INDEX

A

ampullae of Lorenzini 21

B

basking shark 8-9, 18-19
blind shark 14-15

C

chain catshark 17, 18

D

dwarf lanternshark 17, 19

F

filter feeding 9

G

gills 9, 22
glow in the dark sharks 16-17
great hammerhead shark 10-11, 19
great white shark 5, 6-7, 18, 21
Greenland shark 5, 14-15, 19

K

kitefin shark 17, 19

M

megalodon 21

N

ninja lanternshark 16, 18

P

parasites 15, 22
pup (young sharks) 21

S

senses 15
shortfin mako shark 20

T

teeth 13, 21
tiger shark 4

W

whale shark 12-13, 18-19

Z

zebra shark 20
zooplankton 8

About the Author

Annabel is a writer and artist based in Cornwall, UK, who writes children's books with a focus on animals and the natural world. She is the author of the *One Planet* series, about Earth and the environment, and *What Can I See in the Wild*?, published by Beetle Books. In her free time, Annabel enjoys drawing, hiking, and gardening. She is never without a good book.

About the Illustrator

Rose is an illustrator, artist and educator from Hereford, UK, now living and working in London. Her mediums of choice are watercolor, gouache, pencil and Procreate.

Picture Credits

(abbreviations: t = top; b = bottom; c = centre; l = left; r = right)

shutterstock: Wildestanimal 20tr; Andrea Izzotti 20br; Nicola Svoisin44 2tr; Sergey Novikov 21cl; Mark Kostich 21br.

Every effort has been made to trace the copyright holders, and we apologise in advance for any unintentional omissions. We would be pleased to insert the appropriate acknowledgments in any subsequent edition of this publication.